WORLD BOOK'S
CELEBRATIONS AND RITUALS AROUND THE WORLD

World Book, Inc.

a Scott Fetzer Company

Chicago

This edition published in the United States of America
by World Book, Inc., Chicago.
WORLD BOOK and the GLOBE DEVICE are registered
trademarks or trademarks of World Book, Inc.

World Book, Inc.
233 North Michigan Avenue,
Chicago, IL 60601 U.S.A.

For information about other World Book publications,
visit our Web site **http://www.worldbook.com** or
call **1-800-WORLDBK (967-5325).**
For information about sales to schools and libraries, call
1-800-975-3250 (United States); **1-800-837-5365 (Canada)**.

2005 Revised printing
Copyright © 2003, McRae Books Srl
Via dei Rustici, 5—Florence, Italy.
info@mcraebooks.com

**The Library of Congress has catalogued the earlier edition of
this title as follows:**

Harvest celebrations.
   p. cm. —(World Book's celebrations and rituals around the
world)
   Summary: Describes how the harvest festival is celebrated in
different countries, by different cultures, and with different foods
around the world when crops are gathered to feed a community.
Includes recipes and activities.
   ISBN: 0-7166-5007-X
   1. Harvest festivals—Juvenile literature. [1. Harvest festivals.
2. Festivals. 3. Holidays] I. World Book, Inc. II Series.
GT4380 .H37 2003
394.264--dc21
                                                    2002027036

ISBN (this edition): 0-7166-5023-1

Printed and bound in China by C&C Offset Printing Co., Ltd.

2 3 4 5 6 7 8 9 10 09 08 07 06 05

McRae Books:
Publishers: Anne McRae and Marco Nardi
Series Editor: Loredana Agosta
Graphic Design: Marco Nardi
Layout: Sebastiano Ranchetti
Picture Research: Laura Ottina, Loredana Agosta
Cutouts: Filippo delle Monache, Alman Graphic Design
Text: Matilde Bardi pp. 7–11, 26–27; Catherine Chambers pp.
40–41; Anita Ganeri pp. 12–21;
Claire Moore pp. 32–33, 42–43; Cath Senker pp. 22–25, 28–31,
38–39; Paige Weber pp. 34–37

Illustrations: Inklink Firenze, Studio Stalio (Alessandro Cantucci,
Fabiano Fabbrucci, Andrea Morandi, Ivan Stalio), MM Illustrazione
(Manuela Cappon and Valeria Grimaldi) Antonella Pastrorelli, Paola
Ravaglia, Paula Holguin, Lorenzo Cecchi

Color Separations: Litocolor, Florence (Italy)

World Book:
Editorial: Paul Kobasa, Lisa Kwon, Maureen Liebenson
Research: Cheryl Graham, Lynn Durbin
Text Processing: Curley Hunter, Gwendolyn Johnson
Proofreading: Anne Dillon

Acknowledgements
The Publishers would like to thank the following photographers
and picture libraries for the photos used in this book.
t=top; tl=top left; tc=top center; tr=top right; c=center; cl=center
left; cr=center right; b= bottom; bl=bottom left; bc=bottom
center; br=bottom right
A.S.A.P Picture Library: 28c, 28b, 29cl, 29br; Corbis/ De Bellis 21tr;
Corbis/ Grazia Neri 25; Dinodia 21cl, 23bl; Farabola Foto: 10t,
12b; Lonely Planet Images: Greg Elms 20t, 23br; Kraig Lieb 25tr;
Francis Linzee Gordan 40cr; Adriadne Van Zandberaen 41tr;
Ross Barnett 42cl; Peter Hines 42cr; Marco Lanza: 25b, 37tr;
Marco Nardi/McRae Books Archives: 12cl, 12tr; The Image Works:
6cl, 6cr, 14tl,15c, 15bl, 16t, 17tr, 18b, 19t, 23t, 24c, 31c, 31b, 32b,
34c, 35tr, 35c, 36c, 37tl, 37cr, 38c, 41b, 43tr; Worldbridges Tibet
24b (http://worldbridges.com/tibet/links.html)

In the same series:

● WORLD BOOK'S
CELEBRATIONS AND RITUALS AROUND THE WORLD

HARVEST
CELEBRATIONS

Table of Contents

Harvest Celebrations

Introduction

Since ancient times, the harvest festival has ranked as one of the most joyful of all holidays. The well-being of families as well as the communities they lived in depended on an abundant gathering of grains and other crops. Many societies tried to ensure a good harvest by honoring their gods and goddesses and celebrating as the crops were sown. Most held at least one thanksgiving festival when the harvest was safely gathered. Today, farmers, and the city-dwellers who depend on the crops they produce, continue to celebrate the harvest in interesting and colorful ways and to thank their gods and goddesses for their bounty. In the United States and Canada, harvest festival is celebrated as Thanksgiving Day.

This Nigerian woman is winnowing grain that she later will grind into flour and then use to bake bread. *Today, about half of the world's population lives in cities. But up until about 100 years ago, most people lived in the countryside and earned their living as farmers.*

Cornhusk masks *like the one above left were worn by the American Iroquois people during festivals. The Iroquois celebrated a number of festivals of thanksgiving during the year.*

At the first New England Thanksgiving, celebrated by the Pilgrim settlers in America, *the settlers thanked God for their survival in their new land. They also thanked the American Indians who taught them how to farm there.*

HARVEST FESTIVALS AROUND THE WORLD

BAISAKHI: In northern India

CHUSOK: The biggest holiday in Korea

DOZYNKI: Polish festival

THE GUELAGUETZA: In Mexico

KAAMATAN: In Malaysia

KWANZAA: African harvest festival

MAKAHIKI: Hawaiian celebration of peace and rebirth

POSVICENI AND OBZINKY: In the Czech Republic

OKTOBERFEST: German folk festival

ONAM: In India

PONGAL: Hindu celebration

PU: In Pakistan

SUKKOT: Seven-day Jewish festival

TET TRUNG THU: In Vietnam

ZHONG QIU: Chinese moon festival

A sheaf of wheat symbolized Demeter, the ancient Greek goddess of agriculture.

In Mesopotamia, people made offerings of the first fruits of the harvest at the temple to the local gods and goddesses. This ancient vase shows a boat in a harvest procession.

The Ancient World

A successful harvest was essential for early farming communities, which produced all their own food. If farmers failed to bring in enough grain, the people could easily go hungry or even starve in the coming year. Because most people believed that the weather and other natural events on Earth were controlled by gods and other supernatural forces, they tried to please these forces by holding ceremonies before or during the planting season and at harvesttime. Some societies, like the Aztecs in ancient Mexico, even made human sacrifices in an attempt to please the gods. Others were content to offer the gods the first or choicest portions of the harvest.

Mesopotamia

Scientist believe the Mesopotamians were the first to plant crops, care for them as they grew, and then harvest them when ripe. Farming allowed the Mesopotamians to accumulate wealth, build cities, and ultimately to create the world's first great civilization.

Ancient Egypt

In ancient Egypt, a great harvest festival was held at the beginning of the season of shemu. It lasted several days and was dedicated to the fertility god Min. During celebrations, the pharaoh cut the first wheat of the harvest with a special sickle and offered it to the god.

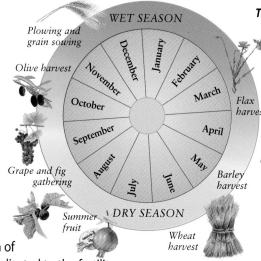

The agricultural calendar in Mesopotamia was divided into the wet season and the dry season. The main harvest of wheat and barley took place at the beginning of the dry season, from late April to early June. Other crops were harvested at different times of the year. This diagram shows the main crops and when they were gathered.

Ancient Celebrations

This Egyptian wall-painting shows a man and his wife carrying out farming chores throughout the year. The Egyptian calendar was divided into three seasons: akhet, the flood; peret, sowing; and shemu, harvest.

Ancient Greece

Ancient Greeks held many festivals to ensure or celebrate a good harvest. Most of them honored Demeter, the goddess of agriculture. The festival of Thesmophoria took place around November, just before farmers sowed the next year's crops. It lasted several days and only women could take part. Another festival, called Thalysia, was held in the summer soon after the wheat harvest. Sacrifices were offered to Demeter to thank her for her bounty.

The Greek goddess Demeter *usually appears holding a sheaf of wheat or a basket of fruit and flowers.*

Roman Sacrifice

In ancient Rome, celebrations dedicated to Ceres, the Roman goddess of agriculture, took place. A spring festival in April lasted for eight days, culminating with Cerealia. Fasting, sacrifices, sports, parades, and feasting were all part of the celebrations. At a festival in August, the Romans offered the first products of the harvest to Ceres. On October 4, a fast was kept in honor of Ceres. Fasting instead of feasting during a religious celebration was rare among the ancient Romans.

THE ENGLISH WORD *CEREAL* comes from *Ceres,* the name of the Roman goddess of agriculture.

Ceres, the Roman goddess of agriculture, *was also associated with pigs. Romans often sacrificed a sow before the start of the harvest.*

Many of the people of ancient Mexico worshiped a corn god, *like the Zapotec god shown here. His chest ornaments were carved in the shape of ears of corn.*

This Aztec image shows the young Xilonen, goddess of young corn. *The Aztecs honored several corn goddesses who represented corn at various stages of growth.*

Pre-Columbian Farmers

The peoples of what is now Mexico and South America cultivated such plants as corn, beans, peppers, tomatoes, and squash. Farther south in the Andes, potatoes were grown. Like all ancient farmers, Pre-Columbian people held ceremonies to ensure good crops and to thank the gods for a successful harvest.

The Aztecs

The Aztecs held many celebrations dedicated to agricultural deities. Cinteotl, a goddess of corn, was honored during a festival held in September. Each year a woman was chosen to represent the goddess. She was dressed in beautiful clothes and honored as if she was a goddess. Later, she was sacrificed to Cinteotl.

PRE-COLUMBIAN refers to the time, people, and events of the period before the explorer Christopher Columbus arrived in America.

This stone head shows the Celtic god Mabon. Mabon was also the name of a Celtic harvest festival that fell on September 22 or 23.

Through History

Many of the harvest festivals we know today have ancient roots. Some, like the Peruvian Sun Festival, are still celebrated much as they were hundreds of years ago. Other celebrations have changed over the centuries or have come to include customs that were once associated with older, or even forgotten festivals that had been held about the same time of the year.

This illustration shows the Virgin Mary on a cloud and a group of angels lifting her to heaven.

This powerful Inca sun mask shows how deeply these ancient people held the sun god in awe. The Inca believed that eclipses of the sun occurred when the god was angry.

The Inti Raymi (Sun Festival) is reenacted in Peru today. On June 24, people gather at archaeological sites and repeat the ancient ritual. Some parts of the ceremony have changed. For example, the llama sacrifice now uses a symbolic animal rather than a real one. The celebrations continue for many hours and include dancing, chanting, and feasting.

August 15

For the Eastern Orthodox and Roman Catholic churches, August 15 is an important feast day dedicated to the Virgin Mary. It is known as the Day of Assumption because members of these churches believe that on that day Mary was taken up (assumed) to heaven. Historians believe that this celebration replaced a much more ancient celebration of the end of summer harvest known as the Feast of Our Lady of the Harvest.

The Inca

For the ancient Inca, Inti Raymi (Sun Festival) was the most important celebration of the year. It was held at about the time of the winter solstice in the Southern Hemisphere (June 20, 21, or 22), at the end of the potato and corn harvests. The sun was the supreme Inca god, and they honored him by offering up a golden tumbler filled with corn beer. Then they sacrificed a llama, and the high priest produced "sacred fire" by shining the rays of the sun onto a golden medallion.

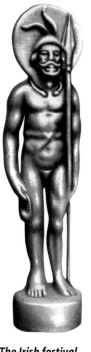

Zoroastrians call the celebration of any gratefully recalled event a Jashan. They hold several Jashans to give thanks for earthly blessings during the agricultural year. This tray holds the offerings that might be made during a Jashan.

Zoroastrianism

The Zoroastrian religion originated in ancient Persia between 1400 and 1000 B.C. Zoroastrians are known as Parsis in India, where most of them now live. They follow a god called Ahura Mazda (Wise Lord). Zoroastrians believe that Ahura Mazda's teachings were revealed through a prophet called Zoroaster and are preserved in a sacred scripture called Avestra.

The Irish festival Lughnasad was celebrated as the feast of the marriage of the god Lugh, above.

Lughnasad

The Celts celebrated their first harvest of the year on August 1 with the Lughnasad festival. Games and sports honored the god Lugh. During the Middle Ages, this festival was taken over by the Christian Church and became known as Lammas, which means loaf-mass. On this day, people baked loaves of bread using the first grains harvested. Then people took them to church to be blessed.

During the Middle Ages, the Archangel Michael, left, *was honored as the protector of God's people.*

THE PAGAN CALENDAR AND FALL EQUINOX

The fall equinox occurs on September 22 or 23 in the Northern Hemisphere. Solstices and equinoxes are solar events, and they have to do with Earth's position in relation to the sun at different times of the year. The moments each year when the sun is at its northernmost or southernmost position in the sky are the two yearly solstices. The exact date differs each year. One occurs on June 20, 21, or 22, and the other on December 21 or 22. The equinox is either of two days when day and night are the same length all over the world. They occur on March 19, 20, or 21 and on September 22 or 23. These days have been important in many traditions, including European pagan ones.

This painting by Peter Brueghel of a peasant wedding in Europe during the Middle Ages includes images of the last sheaves of the harvest. Peasants hung the sheaves throughout the winter, because they believed this would ensure a rich harvest the following year.

Harvest Feasts in the Middle Ages

In medieval Europe, much of the harvest was completed by the end of September. Farmers had time to think about the past year and consider the approaching winter. In Britain, the Michaelmas feast day on September 29, in celebration of the Archangel Michael, was a time for paying annual dues, signing new leases, and rendering accounts. Traditional feasts included fattened goose. Many people still have goose on Michaelmas, which some churches celebrate on November 8. Martinmas, held on November 11, celebrated St. Martin of Tours. Since food was plentiful after the harvest, there was feasting and drinking as well as storytelling and such sporting events as racing and wrestling.

The yin-yang symbol *reflects a traditional Chinese belief that the moon, ruled over by Chang E, is female (yin), and the sun, ruled over by her husband, is male (yang).*

Celebrating Zhong Qiu

The Festival of the Harvest Moon is celebrated with moon gazing, fireworks displays, and special foods. Children are allowed to stay up later than usual to watch the full moon rise. Homes and streets are decorated with thousands of colorful paper lanterns to remind people of the moon. A highlight of the festival is a grand lantern parade through the streets. Moon altars are also set up, laden with offerings of melons and other round foods.

Festival of the Moon in China

In midautumn, the Chinese celebrate Zhong Qiu, one of the most important festivals in the Chinese calendar. It is also called the Festival of the Harvest Moon. It takes place on the 15th day of the 8th lunar month, usually in September, when the moon is at its fullest in the night sky. Some people sit up all night admiring the moon's beauty. The round shape of the moon represents togetherness. People come from far and wide to be reunited with their families and to enjoy a delicious festival dinner. It is also an important occasion for celebrating the harvest and all the good things it brings.

Children walk on stilts, *play games, and watch puppet shows during Zhong Qiu.*

Chang E flies to the moon, *away from her husband, Hou Yi, the archer.*

THE FAR EAST

The Far East is the easternmost part of Asia. Asia extends from Africa and Europe in the west to the Pacific Ocean in the east. The northernmost part of the continent is in the Arctic. In the south, Asia ends in the tropics near the equator. Traditionally, the term Far East has referred to China, Japan, North Korea, South Korea, Taiwan, and eastern Siberia in Russia. Southeast Asia includes Borneo, Brunei, Cambodia, East Timor, Indonesia, Laos, Malaysia, Myanmar, the Philippines, Singapore, Thailand, and Vietnam.

The Lady in the Moon

There are many legends about Zhong Qiu. One tells the story of Hou Yi, a famous archer, who was given the pill of immortality as a reward. But his wife, Chang E, found the pill and tasted it out of curiosity. It caused her to float into the air and up to the moon, where she still lives. Hou Yi built a palace on the sun. Once a year, on the 15th day of the 8th month, he visits his wife, which is why the moon is at its brightest then.

A Chinese victory over the Mongols is remembered each year by eating moon cakes. According to one legend, moon cakes helped to save China from its enemies.

Legend of the Moon Cakes

Special round cakes called moon cakes are baked for Zhong Qiu. The cakes may be stamped with a picture of a hare, which the Chinese say you can see in the moon. According to legend, centuries ago, China was invaded and conquered by the armies of the Mongols. Later, when the Chinese began a rebellion to overthrow the Mongols, moon cakes were baked with messages inside. These were smuggled secretly to the people, telling them when to launch their attack.

Farmers bring in the rice harvest.

An exciting dragon dance is a highlight of the Moon Festival.

Legend says that the ancient Chinese emperor Shennong, the divine farmer, taught the Chinese to grow crops.

Around the World

Zhong Qiu is one of the happiest holidays in the Chinese year. It is celebrated in China, Taiwan, Hong Kong, Singapore, and other countries where Chinese people have settled. In Taiwan, Zhong Qiu is a time for families to come together and to worship in the temples. After dusk, people also picnic under the stars.

THE HOLY FARMER

Many people think the Moon Festival originally was held to mark the safe harvesting of the crops in the fall, at the time of the full moon. It was a time for people to enjoy themselves after the hard work of harvesting and to give thanks to the gods for the crops. The mythical emperor, Shennong (also known as Yan Di), was the god of agriculture and medicine. Stories say he taught the Chinese people how to farm the land and grow crops for food. He also taught people how to treat illnesses using plants as medicines.

Vietnam, Korea, and Japan

Rice offerings are made at the Japanese rice harvest. Leftover rice stalks are made into bundles and offered to Inari, the god of rice.

Midautumn is an important time for farmers in the Far East. Many festivals are held at this time to thank the gods for a good harvest and to ask for their blessings in the coming year. In many places, this is also a time for honoring the ancestors. People visit and clean their ancestors' graves and leave offerings of freshly harvested food. Afterward, they enjoy special feasts with friends and family, dancing, and traditional games. In Korea, the harvest festival is called Chusok. It is the biggest holiday of the year. In Vietnam, fall brings the festival of Tet Trung Thu. Japan has several harvest festivals, particularly celebration of the rice harvest.

A shop in Saigon, Vietnam, overflows with lanterns and toys at Tet Trung Thu.

AT TET TRUNG THU, children make or buy colorful lanterns in many shapes, including dragons, unicorns, hares, boats, birds, and stars. In the evening, children place candles inside the lanterns and carry them in a procession through the streets, to the sound of drums and cymbals. Some say the glowing lanterns represent the brightness of the moon as it lights up the dark night. They also express the wish for the return of the sun's warmth.

MAKE A LANTERN

- two 8 ½ x 11 inch sheets of construction paper
- a ruler
- a pencil
- scissors
- one 8 ½ x 11 inch sheet of colored tissue paper
- glue or a stapler
- a small flashlight or chemical light stick (optional)

Fold the construction paper in half lengthwise. With a ruler and pencil, draw lines about an inch apart along the fold. Cut slits along the lines, leaving a 1-inch margin at the open edges of the paper. Unfold and then paste or staple the edges together (widthwise) to create the lantern. Staple or glue the tissue paper edges together (widthwise) to make a tube. Staple or glue it to the inside of the lantern. Cut a strip of construction paper (about 1 x 8 inches) and glue it to the inside of the lantern to make the handle. Place your lantern on a table or counter. Put a small flashlight or chemical light stick inside the lantern to make it shine.

Tet Trung Thu

The Vietnamese festival of Tet Trung Thu is similar to China's Festival of the Harvest Moon (see pages 12–13). It also falls on the 15th day of the 8th lunar month and celebrates the beauty of the full moon. Families get together to honor their ancestors, gaze at the moon, and enjoy delicious moon cakes. It is a particularly special time for children, with spectacular unicorn and dragon dances in the streets.

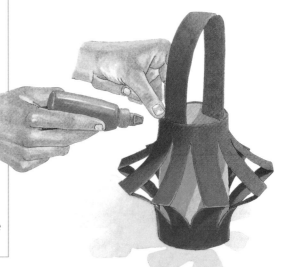

Chusok Food and Clothes

Koreans enjoy many special foods at Chusok. The most famous are called songpyon. These are crescent-shaped rice cakes stuffed with roasted sesame seeds, red bean or chestnut paste, or honey. They are traditionally steamed over pine needles. People offer songpyon to their ancestors. They place rice cakes made with newly harvested rice and freshly picked fruits on the graves. In return, they believe their ancestors will protect them and bless them with good fortune and prosperity. People also wear traditional Korean clothing. Women wear long, wrap-around skirts and short jackets. Men wear baggy trousers and somewhat longer jackets.

These Korean girls are wearing hanboks. A woman's hanbok includes a short, chest-length jacket called a chogori and a full wrap-around skirt called a ch'ima. A man's hanbok includes a longer chogori and baggy trousers called paji. This ceremonial clothing dates back to the Choson Dynasty (1392–1910).

The mask-dance drama is a Korean folk art that has been passed down through many generations and festivals. Expressive masks and colorful costumes bring the characters to life.

Chusok Fun and Games

The Korean harvest festival of Chusok usually falls in September. People start the day by visiting the graves of their ancestors and performing ceremonies to honor them. Then the games begin. Activities may include mask dances, an ancient circle dance called ganggangsuwollae (also spelled kanggangsuwollae), and tug-of-war. The circle dance is performed by girls, traditionally by the light of the full moon. Centuries ago, when Korea was threatened by invasion, women formed rings around campfires on hilltops to make the invaders think the number of soldiers was larger than it actually was. One of the most popular events is the tortoise play. Two men dress up as a tortoise and tour the town, dancing and singing in return for food and drink.

A torii is a gateway to a Shinto shrine. It separates the sacred world from the outside world.

Inari's messenger is a fox, and his shrines are guarded by a pair of stone foxes.

Harvesttime in Japan

Japanese farmers traditionally performed private thanksgiving ceremonies at the end of the harvest, when the ta no kami (god of the rice fields) was believed to leave the fields. Farmers welcomed the ta no kami from the fields into their homes and displayed rice plants and other offerings there for the god. In some places, entire villages gathered to give thanks for a successful harvest.

A portable shrine, or mikoshi, is paraded through the streets in a thanksgiving procession for the rice harvest.

God of Rice

Inari is the Shinto god of rice and the rice fields. Shinto is the ancient religion of Japan. Inari is sometimes shown as a bearded man sitting on a white fox.

Celebrating the Rice Harvest

In many parts of the Far East, rice is the most important food. In Thailand, the Philippines, and Malaysia, people celebrate the rice harvest in April or May with many colorful celebrations and festivals. These are times for giving thanks for the rice crop and looking forward to a new planting season. Many legends, customs, and rituals are associated with the festivals. In Thailand, the annual Royal Plowing Ceremony marks the official start of the rice-planting season and represents farmers' hopes for a successful harvest.

A mask from Borneo is used to keep away evil spirits and hide a person's identity during the harvest festival.

The Royal Plowing Ceremony was revived by the Thai government in 1960 in accordance with the king's wish that a day be dedicated to Thai farmers.

The Royal Plowing Festival

In Thailand, the rice-planting season starts with the Royal Plowing Festival. This ancient festival is held in a large field near the Grand Palace. The Lord of the Plowing Ceremony performs various rituals. Two sacred oxen turn a few furrows with a red-and-gold sacred plow, then the rice is ceremonially scattered. Farmers try to gather a few of the seeds to mix with their own seed. They hope that this will bring them good luck in the next harvest.

After plowing, the sacred oxen are offered seven types of rice and other food from gold and silver baskets. Tradition says that whatever the oxen choose to eat will be plentiful the following year.

Kaamatan in Malaysia

The Kadazan (also called Dusun) people of Sabah, Malaysia, celebrate a harvest festival called the Kaamatan in May. This is a time of thanksgiving for the rice harvest and the beginning of the planting season. According to legend, the creator god sacrificed his daughter when food was scarce. Out of her body grew stalks of rice and other plants that saved the people from starvation. The month-long festival is marked with prayers, dancing, feasting, buffalo races, and games.

Kadazan dancers in traditional black silk costumes, with baskets on their backs, prepare to perform the harvest dance.

These houses are decorated with kipping, a type of pahiyas. Kipping are leaf-shaped wafers made from brightly colored rice paste. They are also eaten as snacks.

Pahiyas in the Philippines

The town of Lucban in the Philippines is known for its annual harvest festival, called Pahiyas, held on May 15. For this colorful celebration, people decorate their houses with precious offerings, called pahiyas, from which the festival gets its name. These offerings include rice, vegetables, and fruit. On this day, people go to church. Then they decorate their water buffalo with flowers and ribbons and take them to be blessed. In the evening, families gather for a great feast. Pahiyas is held in honor of St. Isidro (also Isidore) the Farm-Servant, patron saint of farmers. People carry a statue of St. Isidro in a procession through town to church.

St. Isidro was a farmer who lived from about 1070 to 1130. According to legend, while Isidro prayed, his field was plowed by a team of snow-white oxen guided by an angel.

A woman in Bali makes offerings to the gods of the harvest.

Precious Offerings

In Bali and other parts of Indonesia, people make offerings to the gods to ensure a good harvest and bring good luck. The goddess of rice and the harvest is Dewi Sri.

A favorite Pongal story describes how Lord Krishna, above, lifted up Mount Govardhan to shelter his cowherd friends during a terrible storm sent by Lord Indra.

South and Central Asia

Hindu Harvest Festival

A great Hindu harvest festival excites the people of southern India in mid-January. The three-day festival is called Pongal (also known as Makar Sankranti). Pongal is also the name of a sweet rice pudding. The Pongal celebration is a joyful time when people thank God not only for their crops but also for the sun, the earth, and their cattle. It is a time for throwing out the old and welcoming the new. Friends and neighbors share a sumptuous feast to celebrate a successful harvest.

Lord Indra is the Hindu god who rules over the skies and the clouds that give rain to make crops grow.

Making Kolams

The first day of Pongal is called Bhogi pongal. It is dedicated to Lord Indra, god of clouds and rain. This is a family day when houses are cleaned and space prepared for prayers. Colorful designs called kolams are drawn in doorways with a paste made from rice flour. Newly harvested rice, sugar cane, and turmeric (an herb similar to ginger) are gathered in preparation for making pongal pudding the next day.

The yellow pumpkin flower design in the middle of the kolam is a symbol of fertility. Sometimes real flowers are set in balls of cow dung in the center of kolams.

SOUTH AND CENTRAL ASIA

South and Central Asia are areas of distinct cultures and peoples. These regions form an area at the base of Asia. Asia extends from Africa and Europe in the west to the Pacific Ocean in the east. The northernmost part of the continent is in the Arctic. In the south, Asia ends in the tropics near the equator. South Asia is made up of Afghanistan, Armenia, Bangladesh, Bhutan, India, the Maldives, Nepal, Pakistan, Sri Lanka, the Tibetan plateau in southwest China, and parts of the countries of Azerbaijan and Georgia. Much of India, the largest country in south Asia, forms a peninsula that extends southward into the Indian Ocean. Central Asia includes the countries of Kazakhstan, Kyrgyzstan, Tajikistan, Turkmenistan, Uzbekistan, and the West Siberian Plain.

Blessings of the Sun

Surya pongal, the second day of Pongal, is a time for worshiping Surya, the sun god. A piece of wood is placed on the ground and a large image of the sun god drawn on it, surrounded by kolam designs. Then people perform puja (prayers) and make offerings of pongal pudding to the sun god in return for his blessings on the land and harvest.

Surya, the sun god, is pulled through the sky in his chariot by seven white horses.

Pongal falls at the beginning of the month of Thai. *It is believed that if an unmarried girl prays to the gods every day during Thai, she will be blessed with a suitable husband.*

The Boiling Over

The word *pongal* comes from the Tamil word meaning to boil. Sweet rice pudding called pongal is a dish eaten at this festival. It is made in a new pot that is often painted with leaves and tumeric flowers. Sugar cane is crushed and boiled to make jaggery (sugar syrup). Milk is heated until it boils, then the rice and jaggery are added. At one point, the pongal is allowed to boil over and spill out of the pot.

Pongal pudding *is cooked in a new clay pot.*

Decorating Cattle

The third day of Pongal is known as Mattu pongal, or the festival of cattle. For Hindus, the cow is sacred as the giver of nourishing milk. Farmers honor their cattle by painting their horns and decorating them with beads, bells, and flower garlands. The cattle are given pongal pudding to eat.

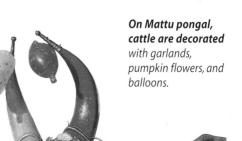

On Mattu pongal, cattle are decorated *with garlands, pumpkin flowers, and balloons.*

Offerings to Agni

At Pongal, some people light bonfires in front of their houses and burn any useless or worn-out things. This symbolizes the cleaning out of the old and the bringing in of the new.

Agni, the fire god, *right, carries messages between human beings and the gods.*

Women carry flames *as part of a Pongal celebration.*

Other Festival Bonfires

Around the time of Pongal, people in Assam, in eastern India, celebrate Bhogali Bihu. They offer prayers to Agni, god of fire. They also build tall wooden structures called meji and set fire to them. In Punjab in northwestern India, many people celebrate Lohri. It marks the end of winter and the harvesting of crops. Children go from house to house, collecting firewood and donations for a big bonfire. In the evening, everyone gathers around the bonfires. People throw harvest products, such as sugar cane stalks, sesame seeds, and parched rice, into the fire as offerings and ask for blessings.

India, Bhutan, and Pakistan

In India and the rest of southern Asia, harvest festivals take place at different times of the year, depending on a region's crops. The popular 10-day festival of Onam occurs at the end of the monsoon season, in August or September. Hindus, Muslims, and Christians alike celebrate Onam in the southwestern Indian state of Kerala. After prayers and worship, the head of each household presents new clothes to the family. People also decorate their homes with flowers and lights. A great feast is prepared, and food is distributed to the poor and needy. Games, music, and dancing are all part of the festivities.

During Onam, conch shells are blown to accompany the snake-boat races.

During the 10 days of Onam, people in Kerala enjoy parades, carnivals, and colorful fireworks displays. The man shown above wears a King Mahabali costume.

Celebrating Onam

At Onam, thousands of people flock to the riverbank to watch the snake-boat races. Long, graceful boats, decorated with flags and umbrellas, are rowed along by as many as 100 men who sing traditional boating songs. The races are fast and furious and make an exciting spectacle. Crews train for months to get ready for the races.

The snake-shaped boats are oiled with fish oil, coconut shell, and soot mixed with egg to help them skim smoothly through the water. Only men are allowed on board.

THE STORY OF ONAM

At Onam, people remember the story of King Mahabali, a legendary ruler of Kerala. Mahabali was wise and just and loved by everyone. But the gods became jealous. Lord Vishnu, disguised as Vamana the dwarf, visited the king. He banished Mahabali to the underworld but allowed him to return once a year to visit his loyal subjects. At Onam, people honor his memory.

Festivals of Bhutan

At harvesttime in Bhutan, many people dress in their best clothes and visit the country's Buddhist monasteries. They offer prayers for a good harvest and protection against evil spirits. At some monasteries, the monks perform ancient ceremonial dances. The dances start in the morning and continue until late afternoon. They tell the story of the victory of good over evil.

Dancers from Bhutan wear elaborate masks and costumes that represent the gods and spirits.

This monastery in Bhutan is the focus of local festivals.

Harvest Celebrations in Pakistan

The Kalasha people in northwest Pakistan have their own ancient religion and culture. Their colorful festivals include the fall festival of Pu, which is held in the town of Biriu during October to celebrate the grape and walnut harvest.

A Sikh prays in preparation for the ceremony to join the Khalsa.

A Kalasha woman wears traditional dress.

Sikh Celebrations

In April, Hindus and Sikhs in northern India celebrate the festival of Baisakhi (also spelled Vaisakh). The festival is a time of relaxation before the hard work of harvesting the wheat crop. Baisakhi is especially important for Sikhs. On Baisakhi in 1699, the great Sikh teacher Guru Gobind Singh founded the Sikh Khalsa (brotherhood).

In procession to mark Baisakhi, men carry the Granth Sahib (the Sikhs' holy book) to a place of honor, where it will be read.

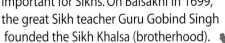

Sukkot

During Sukkot, Jewish people build an outdoor hut called a sukkah. It is symbolic of the temporary shelters their ancestors slept in as they traveled through the desert from Egypt to Canaan (the region later called Israel) and of how God protected them. The sukkah must have at least three sides. The roof is covered with leafy branches or straw and is left partly open to the sky. Inside, people hang fruit, wheat, flowers, and other decorations. Sukkot is also a festival to thank God for the harvest.

During Sukkot, four plants—a palm branch, myrtle, willow, and an etrog, above—are waved in all four directions to show God is present in all four corners of the world.

Altars like this one made of limestone were used to make offerings.

Sukkot in Biblical Times

In Biblical times, Israelites came to the Temple in Jerusalem three times a year for the pilgrim festivals. Sukkot was the third festival. Traditionally, farmers would bring the first fruits of the harvest to be offered in the Temple in Jerusalem.

Wandering in the Wilderness

According to the Bible, Moses led the Israelites out of slavery in Egypt. They wandered through the desert for 40 years until they reached their old homeland of Canaan (later called Israel).

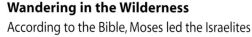

This illustration shows Israelites gathering manna, described in the Bible as a "fine, flaky substance."

Manna from Heaven

The years in the desert were difficult and dangerous. The Israelites and their leader, Moses, argued frequently, and some people rebelled against him. The people complained about the hardships of the journey, the lack of food and water, the dangers, and enemy peoples. The Bible also tells how God offered divine protection through Moses. For example, God provided the Israelites with quails and manna—a miraculous food that kept them from starving. Moses also worked wonders to produce water in the desert.

THE MIDDLE EAST

The Middle East covers parts of northern Africa, southwestern Asia, and southeastern Europe. Scholars disagree on which countries make up the Middle East. But many say the region consists of Bahrain, Cyprus, Egypt, Iran, Iraq, Israel, Jordan, Kuwait, Lebanon, Oman, Qatar, Saudi Arabia, Sudan, Syria, Turkey, United Arab Emirates, and Yemen. The region also is the birthplace of three major religions—Judaism, Christianity, and Islam.

Festivities in the Sukkah

Jewish people still build sukkahs. On the eve of the festival, a palm branch, myrtle, willow, and an etrog (called the four species) are brought to the synagogue, where they are waved during the service. Wine is blessed, then everyone goes home to their sukkah. There, the wine is blessed again, and everyone washes their hands. The worshipers eat a festive meal, normally in the sukkah. Some people, particularly those in Israel, spend the whole festival living in the sukkah.

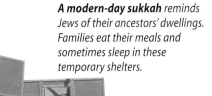

A modern-day sukkah reminds *Jews of their ancestors' dwellings. Families eat their meals and sometimes sleep in these temporary shelters.*

At a Sukkot service at the Western Wall in Jerusalem, men hold the four species.

Worshipers always wash their hands before praying. They also wash them before a festive meal as a symbol of religious purity.

HOW TO MAKE A SUKKAH DECORATION

• a wire clothes hanger
• colored tissue paper
• twist ties
• twigs, branches, leaves, flowers, acorns, autumn fruits
• string
• colored construction paper and scissors (optional)

Cut approximately 10 strips of tissue paper (about 1 inch wide and 12 inches long) and wrap them around the coat hanger. Wrap the branches and twigs around the hanger and fasten them with the twist ties. Cut the string in varying lengths. Tie one end of each piece of string to the leaves, acorns, or flowers. Tie the other end to the hanger. Alternatives to real leaves or fruits are leaf and fruit shapes cut from colored construction paper. Hang the mobile from the roof of the sukkah.

Ornaments called keters or crowns, above, are found in synagogues. They are placed on top of the Torah scrolls. At Shavuot, the Jewish people commemorate the gift of the Torah.

AT SHAVUOT, devout Jews go to synagogue in the evening, when the festival starts. They recite a psalm and hear the story of how God gave the Torah to the Israelites. The Ten Commandments are read. People stay up all night studying the Torah, then recite the morning prayer at dawn. Young children are often given their first Bible storybooks at Shavuot.

This painting of Moses shows him holding up tablets with the Ten Commandments.

Shavuot

Like Sukkot, Shavuot marks both an event in the history of the Jewish people and a season in the farming year. Shavuot commemorates the time when God revealed himself to Moses on Mount Sinai and gave him the Ten Commandments. The word *Shavuot* means weeks in Hebrew. The festival is also known as the Feast of Weeks, because it begins seven weeks (a week of weeks) after the start of Passover (also called Pesach). Shavuot also celebrates the wheat and barley harvests and the ripening of the first fruits of the year.

In Israel, Shavuot coincides with the start of the wheat harvest. Traditionally, farmers kept the first sheaves of barley and wheat to offer to God at the Temple in Jerusalem.

The Ten Commandments

When Moses and his people reached Mount Sinai, God told Moses to prepare the Israelites for his visit. On the morning of the third day, there was thunder and lightning, and the earth trembled. Mount Sinai was covered with clouds and smoke, and God spoke through the clouds. He gave the people his Ten Commandments. He said they should worship him alone and gave them rules for living. The Ten Commandments are an essential part of the Torah, the first five books of the Bible.

A special calendar is used to count Omer—the days between Passover and Shavuot.

The First Fruits

The festival of first fruits has been celebrated since Biblical times. In those days, Israelite farmers brought offerings to the Temple in Jerusalem. They brought the first wheat and barley and fruits such as grapes, figs, and pomegranates. Today, people decorate their homes and synagogues with plants and flowers.

Counting Omer

The 49-day period between Passover and Shavuot is called Omer. It is traditional to keep count of the days to remember the link between Passover, when the Israelites escaped from Egypt, and Shavuot, when they received the Torah and became truly free. Every night a blessing is recited and the day of Omer is stated.

The Western Wall, also known as the Wailing Wall in Jerusalem, far right, has become a customary place to walk during Shavuot.

CHEESE CAKE

- 1 cup graham cracker crumbs
- 4 tablespoons butter, melted
- 4 tablespoons sugar
- 2 lb. (32 oz.) cream cheese, softened
- 1 cup sugar
- 3 tablespoons all-purpose flour
- 4 eggs
- 1 cup sour cream
- 2 teaspoons vanilla extract
- chopped fresh fruit or melted jelly

In a bowl, combine the crumbs, butter, and sugar for the crust. Grease and flour a 10-inch springform pan and press the mixture into bottom. Bake in a preheated oven at 350 °F for 10 minutes. To make the filling, beat the cream cheese, sugar, and flour until well blended. Add the eggs one at a time, beating well after each addition. Beat in the sour cream and vanilla. Pour the filling over the crust and bake for 1 hour. Turn the oven off and leave the cheese cake inside with the door half open until the cake is cool. Remove from the pan when completely cooled and chill in the refrigerator for 1 to 2 hours. Serve as is or with a melted fruit jelly glaze or chopped fresh fruit.

Special Foods

At Shavuot, Jews traditionally eat dishes containing milk, such as cheese cake and cheese-filled pancakes called blintzes. Some people believe this is because in the Bible, both the Torah and the land of Israel are compared to milk.

Celebration on the Kibbutz

A kibbutz is a type of farm-based Jewish community that exists in Israel. All adult members of the kibbutz have an equal say in how the community is run. No one owns private property. Members work for the kibbutz, which owns the property. In return, they receive the goods and services they require. The first kibbutz was formed in what is now Israel in 1909.

The Book of Ruth

The Book of Ruth is always read at Shavuot. The book is set during the spring harvest season. Ruth, who was not Jewish, married an Israelite from Bethlehem. When he died, she went with her mother-in-law, Naomi, back to Bethlehem. Ruth worked for Boaz, a relative of Naomi's, and they then got married. According to the story, their son was the grandfather of King David, Israel's most famous king.

This scene shows Ruth gathering the leftover barley after the harvest. In the story, she works for Naomi's relative, Boaz, who is a rich farmer.

A group of young people celebrates Shavuot on a kibbutz.

France and United Kingdom

In France, the main harvest festival, usually held in November, celebrates the grape harvest and the tasting of the new season's wine. Villagers spill out onto the streets to share a glass of wine, and to feast and dance. The harvest is still widely celebrated in rural areas of the United Kingdom. In the United Kingdom, celebrations take place in September, around the time of the harvest moon. Usually, farmers bring produce to lay on the altar during a church service. Afterward, the congregation may go to the village hall for a harvest supper. The local women spend the days leading up to the feast day cooking.

Bunches of grapes hang heavier on the vines as the summer days shorten into fall in September and October. The fruit for crisp, white wines is harvested first, while grapes for sweet dessert wines are left almost until the first frost.

Winemaking is a very old tradition in France. It was introduced into the country at least 2,000 years ago.

Europe and the Americas

At the Grape Harvest Festival in the region of Alsace in France, people dress in traditional costumes and dance in the streets. The streets are lined with stalls offering the new season's wines.

Rice in France

Rice-growing became important in France during the early 1900's. That's when the French drained the salty water from the marshy lands near where the Rhone River flows into the Mediterranean Sea, a region called Carmaque.

The Grape Harvest Festival

Wine is produced all over France. Many areas are famous for the wines they produce. Champagne produces bubbly wines that are used to celebrate special occasions all over the world. Burgundy and Bordeaux are better known for their red wines. Throughout France, people celebrate the grape festival. Another festival is held when the new wines are ready for drinking.

The Rice Harvest Festival in the Carmaque region of France features locals dressed in folk costumes and parading through the streets when the backbreaking work of harvest is over.

EUROPE

Europe is one of the smallest of the world's seven continents in area but one of the largest in population. Europe extends from the Arctic Ocean in the north to the Mediterranean Sea in the south and from the Atlantic Ocean in the west to the Ural Mountains in the east. The 47 countries of Europe include the world's largest country, Russia, as well as the world's smallest, Vatican City. Russia lies partly in Europe and partly in Asia.

Harvest Home

In the United Kingdom, harvest festivals are called Harvest Home, the Kern, the Ingathering, or the Inning. People celebrate the end of the hard work of harvesting, and the fact that their granaries and pantries are full for the approaching winter. In recent years, many schools have begun to celebrate the harvest. Teachers and pupils bring produce from home and put it in a special room in the school or local church. After the festival, it is given to charity organizations.

*At **Harvest Home in London,** Cockney costermongers (people who sell fruit, fish, and other produce from carts on the streets) celebrate the harvest with a special church service. The man in the foreground is wearing a suit entirely embroidered with buttons.*

HOW TO MAKE CORN DOLLIES

- 6–8 pieces of fresh or dried corn husks
- string
- scissors
- about 4 cotton balls
- glue and scraps of cloth to dress the dollie (optional)
- colored markers (optional)

If you are using dried husks, soak them in water for about 20 minutes to soften. Take a strip of husk and place the cotton balls in the middle. Gather the husk beneath the balls and tie with string to make a neck.

To make the arms, fold another husk and tie it at each end to make the hands. Slip the arm section between the two layers of the main husk. Tie with a string to make a waist. To make a female dollie with a long skirt, cut the husk straight across the bottom. To make a male dollie, cut the skirt in two and tie each leg at the ankles. To make a fancier dollie, use a colored marker to draw on eyes and mouth and glue on pieces of colored cloth for an apron or shirt.

Dollie Traditions

In the United Kingdom, corn dollies were made with the last sheaf of wheat harvested. There, the word *corn* can refer to any type of grain, including wheat and barley. The dolls were kept until spring, because people believed that during harvesting, the wheat spirit withdrew to the last remaining strands of wheat. When these were cut, the spirit was trapped. Keeping the husks kept the wheat spirit alive until the new crop flourished. During winter, the dollies were hung in churches, taverns, farmhouses, or barns. In spring, they were plowed back into the fields. Corn dollies are made in many European countries.

HARVEST CELEBRATIONS IN IRELAND usually take place outdoors or in churches. Potatoes, apples, nuts, and corn are sold, and cornhusking competitions are sometimes held.

German Harvesttime

Celebrations of thanksgiving have a long tradition in the German-speaking parts of Europe, including Germany, Austria, and part of Switzerland. The celebrations are held in churches, marketplaces, homes, and dance halls. In church, people thank God for the harvest. There is no national thanksgiving holiday. But many families, especially in farming communities, have a special harvest thanksgiving feast in the autumn. At this time of year, the cattle are brought home from their summer pastures. Tinkling cowbells announce their arrival. Harvesttime is also when the famous Munich Oktoberfest is celebrated.

Beer *is made from grain, pure water, yeast, and flavorings, such as hops or fruit.*

A harvest thanksgiving procession *in the region of Baden-Württemberg in Germany features women carrying a large festive wreath of wheat and field flowers.*

THE MUNICH OKTOBERFEST, or October Festival, actually begins in September and ends in early October. The chilly winds blowing from the Alps make it too cold to have an outdoor festival later in the fall.

German Thanksgiving

Thanksgiving in the German-speaking countries of Europe is mainly a rural celebration. It is held during early October and varies around the region. People thank God for the harvest of locally grown products, such as grain and fruit. In the Alpine regions, grain is brought into barns on big wagons that are pulled by decorated oxen. Thanksgiving celebrations are fun after the hard work of the harvest. There are dances, parades, banquets, and pageants.

Decorating cows' horns has become an art form. Amazing creations are fixed to the animal's head.

Cows graze in the rich fields of Germany's Black Forest region. Traditionally, cowherds spend the summer in the mountains with the cattle.

When the Cows Come Home

In autumn, people in Alpine areas celebrate the return of the cows or sheep. Local herders drive the cattle or flocks from the mountain pastures, where they have been feeding all summer. The cows are often decorated with flowers or tree branches. They are brought into town in a procession, with their cowbells ringing. Villagers wear national costumes to welcome them. A fair may be held into the night, with feasting, yodeling, and dancing.

A harvest festival pageant in Austria is led by a priest and altar boys. *Girls surround a large harvest garland,* left.

Blessing the Fruits of the Harvest

A harvest thanksgiving service is held in churches on the first Sunday of October. Catholic churches hold a special mass. Beautifully crafted displays of colorful fruit and vegetables, grains, and breads are arranged before the altar. The devout bring fruit and crops to have them blessed. After the service, the produce is donated to needy people in the community. In some areas, people decorate the last sheaf of wheat with colorful ribbons—a pre-Christian tradition. According to tradition, the spirit of the grain is present in the last sheaf harvested.

Crown Prince Ludwig of Bavaria's wedding festivities in 1810 started a festival tradition that became the Oktoberfest.

The traditional way of transporting beer barrels from the breweries is demonstrated at the Oktoberfest.

Oktoberfest

The Oktoberfest in Munich, Germany, takes place each autumn. This festival began as part of a crown prince's wedding celebrations in 1810 and has continued ever since. Now it is the biggest Volksfest (folk festival) in Germany. A procession of local officials and brewers begins the festivities. Vast quantities of beer are sold from giant beer tents. About 1.3 million gallons (about 5 million liters) of beer are poured during the festival! People feast on chicken, veal sausages, trout, and eel grilled outdoors. There is plenty of entertainment, with live music night and day, dancing, and a huge funfair.

Poland, Russia, and the Czech Republic

A Polish harvest wreath is a symbol of the harvested crops. The wreath is kept until the following year, when its grain is added to the seed being sown.

IN MORAVIA, a region in the Czech Republic, an old woman, or the woman who bound the last sheaf of the harvest, is wrapped up in the sheaf herself!

In Poland, Russia, and the Czech Republic, the tradition of celebrating the harvest is still alive but has changed over the years. In Poland, Dozynki was originally a festival sponsored by the lord of the manor for his workers. Today, elected officials, such as the mayor or head of the town council, perform the landlord's role. At some popular festivals in the Czech Republic, people still dress in folk costumes and enjoy traditional music, singing, and food. In Russia, people also celebrate Dozynki. In addition to folk festivals, there are church services during which people offer thanks for the harvest.

At Dozynki, the queen of the harvest wears a crown-shaped wreath made from the finest wheat, rye, oats, and field flowers.

Dozynki in Poland

Dozynki is a traditional Polish harvest festival. In the past, the villagers used to dress in colorful local costumes, then sing and play music. They carried wreaths made from harvested crops as an offering to the local landowner. Nowadays, the ceremony includes everyone in the countryside community. One woman is chosen as queen of the harvest; she parades wearing a harvest crown. People still dress in traditional clothes and carry beautifully made harvest wreaths.

The Dozynki festival includes a lot of singing and dancing. People dance traditional Polish dances to the accompaniment of musicians playing violins, accordions, and clarinets.

The Nanai People

The Nanai live mainly in the lower Amur River Basin in Russia. They also live in China. Until the start of the 1900's, they lived in scattered communities, fishing and hunting. In the 1920's and 1930's, those living in what was the Soviet Union were brought together to live on state-owned farms and farm collectively. Today, they cultivate the land and breed livestock.

Nanai people in Russia celebrate the harvest thanksgiving festival by dressing in traditional costumes and performing a folk dance.

Giving Thanks to Volos

Traditionally in much of eastern Europe, including Russia, the Dozynki celebration was held at the end of the harvest. The last sheaf was brought into the house and decorated with flowers and ribbons or dressed in women's clothes. Centuries ago in Russia, the god of animals and flocks was called Volos (also spelled Veles). Sometimes the last sheaf of wheat was tied in a knot. This was called curling Volos's hair.

The Slavic god of flocks and animals was Volos, below. *Volos was replaced by Saint Vlasii, the protector of the herd, when Christianity spread to Russia.*

These men and women in the Czech Republic wear traditional costumes and prepare for the festivities.

Posviceni and Obzinky

The Czech Republic boasts two harvest festivals—Posviceni and Obzinky. Posviceni is a church festival. Once the harvest is completed, the farm laborers celebrate Obzinky. They make wreaths of wheat or rye and field flowers, then place the wreaths on the heads of the prettiest girls. Everyone enjoys a delicious feast of roast pig, roast goose, and jam- or cheese-filled cakes. After the celebration, the wreaths are kept and hung on walls until the next year.

THE BREADBASKET

Because of its agricultural production, Ukraine became known as the Breadbasket of Europe. Its moderate climate and rich, black soil, called chernozem, have made the country one of the world's most productive farming regions. Ukraine ranks among the leading countries in the production of sugar beets and wheat. Other important crops grown in Ukraine include barley, corn, potatoes, and sunflowers.

American Indian Harvest

Agricultural rites and harvest celebrations have always been an important part of American Indian culture. Some festivities last several days. Many honor rain-bringing gods, and give thanks for good harvests. Among the Hopi people, Kachina dolls play a central role in harvest ceremonies.

In the Great Basin area of western North America, women gathered seeds, nuts, roots, and berries using baskets and beaters like the ones shown here. Ceremonies in late summer and early fall celebrated the harvest of pine nuts, which helped the people survive the winter.

Masks made of corn, above right, *are worn by Iroquois people during several festivals.*

The Hopi make dolls, below, *to represent the kachina spirits.*

The Iroquois people give thanks to the Three Sisters, *also known as Our Sisters. These goddesses protect the corn, bean, and squash crops.*

A Plentiful Harvest

The Iroquois of the Eastern Woodlands were great farmers. They had several festivals during the agricultural year to give thanks for the various crops they cultivated. During the Green Corn Festival in the summer, the Iroquois celebrated the ripening corn. In the fall, they celebrated the harvest, giving thanks for the food they had been provided.

The Kachinas

Many American Indian groups, including the Hopi people of the Southwest, celebrated the corn harvest. The Hopi believed that the kachinas, friendly spirits of departed ancestors, caused the rain to fall and taught the people special skills. During some ceremonial dances, men wore kachina masks to communicate to the spirit world of the kachinas. In midsummer, the Hopi performed a ceremony of thanksgiving for another season of growth.

THE AMERICAS

The continents of North America and South America make up the Western Hemisphere. North America contains Canada, Greenland, the United States, Mexico, Central America, and the Caribbean Sea islands. South America contains Argentina, Bolivia, Brazil (which occupies almost half the continent), Chile, Colombia, Ecuador, Guyana, Paraguay, Peru, Suriname, Uruguay, and Venezuela.

The Hopi used the location of the rising and setting sun over particular landmarks to determine when new seasons began and the right time for ceremonies, planting, and harvesting.

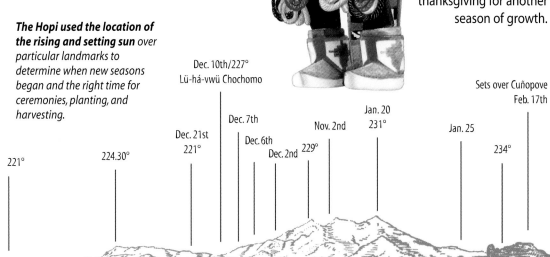

221°

224.30°

Dec. 21st
221°

Dec. 10th/227°
Lü-há-vwü Chochomo

Dec. 7th

Dec. 6th

Dec. 2nd
229°

Nov. 2nd
229°

Jan. 20
231°

Jan. 25

234°

Sets over Cuñopove
Feb. 17th

The Green Corn Festival

Many American Indian groups have performed the Green Corn dance, but it is most closely linked to Indians of the Southeast, such as the Creek. The Green Corn Festival was a time of thanksgiving and purification held just before the harvest. The festival lasted for several days and began with people fasting, praying, and cleaning their homes. The old ceremonial fire was put out and a new one was kindled as a symbol of purification and renewal. The festival continued with singing and dancing. Men and women performed different dances and sometimes danced together. A feast of new corn and other foods ended the ceremony.

American Indians performing the Green Corn dance, usually held in late August.

The Snake Ceremony

The Hopi people believe that all things in nature play a part in maintaining nature's balance. They feel they have a responsibility to keep this balance by having good hearts and performing rituals. The nine-day, colorful Snake Ceremony is performed in late August to bring the rain necessary for a good harvest. Members of the Hopi Snake Society capture snakes, which they handle during the ceremony and then release to carry prayers for rain to the gods.

A feathered headdress, kilt, and snake stick have been used by priests during ceremonies. Snakes symbolize lightning and the rain that follows.

The Prayerstick Festival

Some Pima and Papago people of the Southwest were desert farmers who traditionally cultivated squash, corn, and beans. Earthmaker and Elder Brother were their most important deities, and their ceremonies focused on making the crops grow under dry conditions. Every four years, a harvest festival called the Prayerstick Festival was held, and masked men known as sacred clowns performed ritual dances.

A sacred clown mask of the Papago, above, is decorated with eagle feathers. Holes have been cut for the eyes and mouth.

Thanksgiving History

The cornucopia, also called the horn of plenty, represents abundant food from the land. This symbolic horn comes from the ancient Greek myth of Amalthea, the goat whose milk nurtured the infant god Zeus.

***Aboard the* Mayflower *ship*,** 41 passengers signed the Mayflower Compact, a legal agreement on governing their new colony.

In the autumn of 1621, the Pilgrims of Plymouth, in what is now the state of Massachusetts, invited neighboring natives to a feast to celebrate the Pilgrims' survival in America. The previous year, the American Indians had taught the Pilgrims how to cultivate corn and where to hunt wild turkey and find other foods. At this feast of thanksgiving, Pilgrims and American Indians enjoyed these foods and gave thanks for their good fortune. Though other explorers and settlers had previously held religious services of thanksgiving in America, and American Indian groups had long traditions of thanksgiving ceremonies, this event became the basis for the modern celebration of Thanksgiving Day in the United States.

Captain Miles Standish, the military leader of the Pilgrims, organized the first survey of the new Plymouth Colony in 1620.

The *Mayflower*

The Pilgrims were Puritan Separatists—very strict Protestant Christians who rejected the Roman Catholic and Anglican churches. Persecuted in England for their religious beliefs, they fled to Holland in 1608, but soon decided to start a new community in America. In 1620, investors agreed to finance their new American settlement. That year, 41 members of the group in Holland and 61 other English people sailed on the *Mayflower* from Plymouth, England, to Massachusetts.

The Pilgrims' First Thanksgiving

The Pilgrims' first Thanksgiving lasted for three days in the autumn of 1621. The members of the colony wanted to thank God for their survival. They invited Chief Massasoit and other members of his Wampanoag group to join them. About 90 American Indians came, and they brought five deer to add to the feast.

The Pilgrims had celebrated feasts of thanksgiving in England. Local American Indian groups had celebrated several thanksgiving festivals each year. In 1621, they feasted together.

Martin Frobisher *held a celebration of thanksgiving in what is now Canada in 1578, when he arranged a formal ceremony to thank God for his safe journey from England.*

A National Holiday

In 1859, Canada's Parliament proclaimed November 6 Thanksgiving Day. In 1957, Parliament moved the date to the second Monday in October to match the harvest season. United States President George Washington declared November 26 a day of thanksgiving in 1789. For many years, only some states had a yearly thanksgiving holiday. President Abraham Lincoln declared the fourth Thursday in November a national Thanksgiving Day holiday in 1863. After that, U.S. presidents proclaimed a thanksgiving holiday each year until 1939, when Congress officially made Thanksgiving Day a national legal holiday.

President Abraham Lincoln *declared Thanksgiving Day a national U.S. holiday in 1863.*

Thanksgiving Celebrations in Canada

Canadians celebrate Thanksgiving Day on the second Monday in October. In 1578, the English explorer Martin Frobisher held a religious celebration in what is now Newfoundland to give thanks for his safe journey to America. The French explorer Samuel de Champlain organized a club called the Order of Good Cheer that hosted feasts of thanksgiving.

The French explorer Samuel de Champlain *(1570?–1635) hosted feasts of thanks for his safe explorations of North America. He celebrated with American Indians in what is now Canada.*

Surviving in the New World

The Pilgrims intended to settle in Virginia in 1620, but navigation errors and storms drove the *Mayflower* north to what is now Massachusetts. There they founded Plymouth Colony on land inhabited by American Indians called the Wampanoag. The colonists were unprepared for their new environment, and, at first, many died. American Indian men named Squanto and Samoset, who spoke English, taught the Pilgrims how to cultivate native crops, identify useful plants, and where to find good hunting and fishing.

The Pilgrims who founded Plymouth Colony, below, believed that God had ensured the success of their hard-working settlement. They intended to spread Christian beliefs across America.

King Philip *was the son of the Wampanoag chief Massasoit. His true name was Metacomet. He became chief in 1662.*

King Philip's War

The original Pilgrims were grateful for their help from the Wampanoags, but as the colony grew and prospered, the friendship faltered. A generation later, war broke out. King Philip's War started in 1675, after several years of hostilities. It lasted only a year in some areas, but in other areas, fighting continued until 1678. Hundreds of men, women, and children died on both sides.

Thanksgiving Traditions

American Indians cultivated corn for centuries *before the arrival of the Pilgrims from Europe. The Pilgrims had never seen corn before.*

The turkey *is a native North American bird. At the thanksgiving feast in 1621, guests ate cooked wild turkeys and other wild birds, probably ducks and geese. Today Americans eat nearly 700 million pounds of turkey meat on Thanksgiving Day.*

Today, Thanksgiving Day in the United States is a day to give thanks to God for blessings received during the year. People give thanks with feasting and prayer. Many foods that Americans eat on Thanksgiving Day today were also eaten by the Pilgrims and American Indians at the thanksgiving feast in 1621, including cornbread, turkey, and pumpkin. Athletic competitions also took place then. The Pilgrims and American Indians followed their great feast with races and games. Today, many Americans watch and play football on Thanksgiving Day. They also watch or take part in parades with floats and marching bands.

Feasting with relatives *on Thanksgiving Day is a tradition that evolved from the harvest festivals of ancient times and Christian practices.*

Family Meal

Today, Americans from all cultural and regional backgrounds gather with their families for a Thanksgiving Day feast. Whether the main meal is lunch or dinner, everyone usually eats hearty portions of food. Many people say a prayer before the meal, to thank God for their blessings. A typical Thanksgiving meal includes turkey and stuffing, mashed potatoes, cornbread, cranberry sauce, and pumpkin pie, but menus vary.

The Macy's Thanksgiving Day Parade *in New York City is famous for its huge helium balloons, above. The Christmas shopping season traditionally starts the day after Thanksgiving Day.*

Football, *right, is part of many people's Thanksgiving Day celebration.*

American Festivities

On the morning of Thanksgiving Day, many Americans watch parades, including the Macy's Thanksgiving Day Parade broadcast from New York City. Macy's Department Store launched its parade in 1924. Later Thanksgiving Day, many people watch and play football. The first Thanksgiving Day football game was held in 1876, when the new Intercollegiate Football Association instituted a championship game.

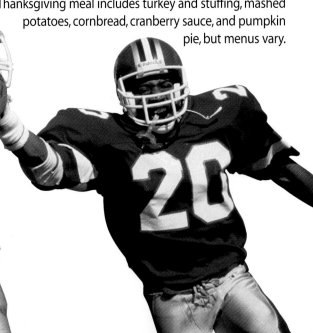

PUMPKIN PIE

- 3 large eggs
- 2 cups freshly cooked or canned pumpkin puree
- 1½ cups light cream
- ¾ cup sugar
- 1 teaspoon each ground cinnamon and ginger
- ½ teaspoon each ground nutmeg and allspice
- ½ teaspoon salt
- 1 unbaked 9-inch pie shell
- whipped cream

Preheat the oven to 375 °F. Whisk the eggs thoroughly in a large bowl. Add all the other ingredients except the pie shell and whipped cream. Continue whisking until well mixed. Pour the pumpkin mixture into the pie shell. Bake for about 35 to 45 minutes. The center of the pie should be set but still quivery if you move the pan. Chill in the refrigerator for up to 1 day. Serve each piece with a dollop of whipped cream on top.

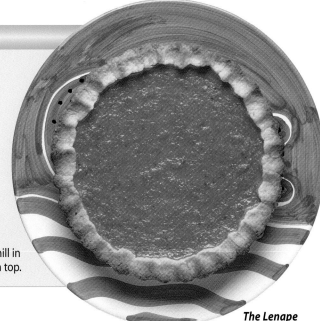

Cranberries

European colonists encountered many new foods in America, including corn, blueberries, and cranberries. For centuries before the colonists' arrival, Indians had harvested cranberries. They made pemmican, a mixture of dried and powdered deer or buffalo meat and fat, and flavored it with berries. They also used berries in dyes and medicine. The colonists called them *crane berries,* because the plant's flowers reminded them of birds called cranes. This name evolved over time into *cranberries.* Historians do not know whether cranberries were served at the thanksgiving feast in 1621.

The Lenape Indians, also known as the Delaware Indians, offered cranberries, far left, *as symbols of peace at group feasts.*

In addition to serving Thanksgiving meals in large dining halls, many charities also deliver food to people who are confined at home because of health or financial problems.

Feeding the Homeless

Many North Americans donate food and other provisions so that people who are homeless or poor can enjoy a full, nutritious Thanksgiving Day meal. Churches, soup kitchens, and civic groups organize food drives for weeks to gather enough food for the meals.

Latin American and Kwanzaa Celebrations

Tuned oil drums, popularly called steel drums, above, *have been played to accompany calypso music. Calypso is a kind of music that originated on the island of Trinidad in the Caribbean Sea.*

At a Kwanzaa feast, the room is decorated in the African colors of red, black, and green. The table holds seven symbolic items: a straw mat, a candle holder, candles, a cup, fruits and vegetables, ears of corn, and gifts.

Latin American celebrations are very diverse. Some, such as the Guelaguetza in Mexico, have ancient origins but were altered when the country was converted to the Roman Catholic form of Christianity. Corpus Christi, a Christian festival commemorating Jesus's Last Supper, is also linked to a celebration of the first fruits. People wearing colorful masks dance in the streets. Great merriment follows the harvest on the island of Barbados. In South America, the Yanomami share the fruits of their harvest with other clans in a gesture of friendship. Kwanzaa, celebrated in the United States, is based on traditional African harvest festivals.

Kwanzaa

Kwanzaa celebrates the African American family, community, and culture. Introduced in 1966, it lasts seven days, from December 26 to January 1. The word *Kwanzaa* comes from the Swahili phrase for first fruits. The celebration centers around seven principles. These principles are Umoja (unity), Kujichagulia (self-determination), Ujima (collective work and responsibility), Ujamaa (cooperative economics), Nia (purpose), Kuumba (creativity), and Imani (faith). It is also a time for celebrating the goodness of life. At Kwanzaa, a candle is lit each day, and children receive gifts.

A colorful street parade, above, *celebrates the Crop Over Festival held during July in Barbados.*

Crop Over

Crop Over is a colorful three-week festival on the island of Barbados. It began several centuries ago as a celebration to mark the end of a successful sugar cane harvest, but the modern celebration dates from about the 1970's. Everyone wears amazing costumes, and there are huge parties called jump-ups. Calypso concerts and competitions are held throughout the festival. The cart parade, stalls, carnival, concerts, and exhibitions attract thousands of visitors from around the world.

A FRIENDLY HARVEST

As a gesture of peace, a Yanomami clan will invite another clan to join them for a feast of produce they have harvested. The Yanomami live in the remote forest of southern Venezuela and northern Brazil. They grow fruit and other crops and hunt animals, such as monkeys and deer.

A group of Yanomami travels to visit neighbors. The group has been invited to share some plantain soup.

MEXICO HAS MANY FESTIVALS. People celebrate national and religious holidays, saints' days, and the local harvest. Nearly every day brings a cause for celebration!

The Dance of the Voladores is performed during Mexico's Corpus Christi celebrations. A man dances atop a 100-foot pole playing the flute. Four others jump from the top and fly around the pole on ropes.

The Guelaguetza

This festival has ancient roots. The native people of what is now the Mexican state of Oaxaca used to sing and dance and make offerings of their harvest to the gods to thank them for good crops. When the Spaniards arrived in 1521, they converted everyone to Catholicism. They combined customs from the older celebrations with a festival day in honor of the Virgin Mary. Nowadays, the main events of the Guelaguetza take place the last two Mondays in July. The celebrations open with a big parade that includes a giant paper lantern called the marmota, people dancing on stilts, and dancers from all over Oaxaca. A contest follows to select a woman to represent the goddess Centeotl. She is not the most beautiful woman but the one who knows her area's history and customs the best. At the Guelaguetza, people wear regional costumes, act out legends, and enjoy wonderful food, crafts, and music.

Dancers perform the pineapple dance at the Guelaguetza.

African Harvest

Africa is a huge continent with vast areas of desert, semi-desert, grassland, and thick forest. As a result, Africans engage in many types of farming and harvest many types of foods. These range from dates and olives in the north to yams and corn farther south. Because Africa is home to many different cultures and religious traditions, harvest is celebrated in various ways. But dance, song, masquerades, and drumming are festive traditions found across much of the continent. So, too, are offerings of food and thanks to God, spirits, and ancestors. Some communities celebrate sowing time as well as the first fruits of the harvest.

Among the Yoruba people, masks play an important cultural role. This mask is used in a ritual masquerade to give thanks for the harvest and ask for the arrival of rains.

Large, decorated gowns like this one worn by a member of the Gelede symbolize the goodness and greatness of the mother goddess among the Yoruba. Striking masks are carved from wood.

New Yams and New Year

The yam harvest, which takes place between August and October, marks traditional New Year in many West African societies. Pestles and mortars used for pounding boiled yams are scrubbed clean before celebrations begin. The first yam may then be offered in thanks to God, the spirits, and ancestors.

A yam is the long, thick base of a stem that grows underground and is called a tuber. It is different from the smaller, rounder sweet potato. Yams can be boiled and mashed. They are also delicious fried or roasted.

Pleasing the Spirits

Across much of Africa, harvest masquerades, dance, and song praise the power and goodness of God and the spirit world. They also remind people that successful farming communities need a strong and lawful society. A secret society called Gelede formed among the Yoruba people of West Africa. The Gelede masquerade, held between March and May, seeks to appease powerful spirits and offers prayers for rain. The Gelede also enact scenes to show the benefits of a well-ordered society.

Young Karo men are transformed into guinea fowl with stippled body painting. Their headdresses are made of ostrich feathers.

AFRICA

Africa lies south of Europe and west of Asia and contains 53 independent countries. Tropical rain forests dominate western and central Africa. The world's largest desert, the Sahara, stretches across northern Africa. Africa also has the world's longest river—the Nile. Much of the continent is grassland. In the north, most of the people are Arabs. The great majority of the African population lives south of the Sahara.

The Karo of Ethiopia

The Karo live along the southwestern edge of the Ethiopian plateau in northeast Africa. They grow mainly root crops, such as yams and sweet potatoes. Celebrations begin after the harvest. The main ceremony is dramatized fighting between the men of local clans. Body and hair decorations are vital to the ritual. As an honor for killing a dangerous enemy or animal, hair is plaited and tied back with glazed earth. The hair and body may then be painted red, white, and black.

The Warrior Dancers

In December, the Swazi people of southern Africa celebrate the royal Incwala festival. Its ceremony is rooted in the story of how, centuries ago, the Swazi people moved to their homeland from a place near the Indian Ocean. The ceremony reconfirms the king's power and is also a festival of the new harvest. About a month before the ceremony, the Swazi king's warriors take a gourd to the sea, fill it with water, and return it to the king. Warriors also collect plants for ceremonial medicines. During the main ceremony, the warriors kill a bull and perform dances. The king eats cleansing medicines and the harvest's first fruits.

Kassena houses are decorated with patterns that symbolize farming. The lines beneath the roof represent the ridges and furrows of earth in which crops are grown.

Swazi warrior dancers wear ceremonial oxhide and leopardskin, above.

Kassena women celebrate the harvest with singing and dancing. Here, some are drumming on calabashes (wooden bowls), which they are also wearing on their heads. Dressed in their best clothes and jewelry, three women, using a carved ladder, watch the dancing from above.

Music of the Kassena

The Kassena live in northern Ghana, a dry part of West Africa. Farmers there grow millet, a grain that does not need much rain. In December, just before the millet harvest, the Kassena celebrate the Fao festival. No one in the village disturbs the crop until the earth priest's son plays a flute made from a ripe millet stem. Then villagers sing, dance, and drum. Food is blessed and taken to the village chief's house.

This mask of the Baining people of Papua New Guinea is used in dances. Different types of masks are used in daytime and nighttime festivals.

Harvest in the Pacific

Among most Oceanic cultures, the yam has been the staple crop for many centuries. It is eaten boiled, roasted, baked, or mashed. Oceanic people also traditionally have performed many elaborate rituals to protect and encourage the yam's harvest. These rituals involve much singing and dancing and the carving of ceremonial masks of various styles and colors. Oceanic harvest festivals, especially in Hawaii, are a time of fun and games and a time to rejoice in the harvest produced.

This artwork is of the head of a feather god. Captain Cook collected many of these on his voyage to Hawaii in the late 1700's.

THE GOD LONO is known in other parts of Oceania as Rongo or Ro'o. He was the god of the harvest and represented peace for the Hawaiian people.

AUSTRALASIA AND OCEANIA

Australasia and Oceania lie east of Asia and west of the Americas. Australasia refers to Australia, New Guinea, New Zealand, and other nearby islands. New Guinea and New Zealand are also considered as part of the Pacific Islands, or Oceania. Oceania is a name given to a group of many thousands of islands scattered across the Pacific Ocean. New Guinea is the largest island in the group. It contains Irian Jaya, which is a part of Indonesia, and the independent country of Papua New Guinea. Islands near the mainland of Asia (Indonesia, Japan, the Philippines) are part of Asia. Islands near North and South America (the Aleutians, the Galapagos) are grouped with those continents. Australia is itself a continent.

LONO AND CAPTAIN COOK

Many people believe that the death of British explorer Captain James Cook is linked to the Hawaiian myth of Lono. In 1778, Cook became the first known European to visit the Hawaiian Islands. His arrival coincided with the Makahiki season. For many Hawaiians, the tall masts and square white sails of his ships looked like the symbol of the god Lono—a tall white staff with a crosspiece from which a white banner hung and which priests and others mounted on their canoes in the Makahiki season. They assumed that Cook was the white-skinned Lono returning to the islands. They took him to the main temple of Lono. Cook left the island before the end of the Makahiki season, as myth said he should. When he returned unexpectedly to repair one of his ships after the Makahiki season was over, the islanders became angry and suspicious. Cook was stabbed and killed during a fight over a stolen boat.

Captain James Cook was killed in Hawaii in 1779.

Makahiki Festival

For the Hawaiian people, the Makahiki season is a time of peace and rebirth following harvest. Native Hawaiians watched for the arrival of the constellation Pleiades above the horizon just after sunset before starting Makahiki festivities. The Makahiki season lasted from October or November until late January or early February. During the holiday, wars and battles ended, taxes were paid to the ruling chiefs, and sports and contests were organized between villages. Thanks were given for the harvest season and prayers offered to the god Lono for bringing the rains. Today, many traditional sports and games are still played during the festival.

Canoe racing is a favorite Hawaiian sport during the Makahiki festival.

Yam Rituals of Papua New Guinea

In Papua New Guinea, each culture has formed its own rituals to protect and celebrate the yam harvest. Often these ceremonies focus on the inseparability of man, yams, and the spirit world. From June to August, the Milamala yam harvest festival is held on many parts of the island. It starts with a procession of men carrying the newly harvested yams from the storage hut to the village yam houses. Sometimes dancing and feasting follow, with the best yams being put on display. In the Washkuk hills of Papua New Guinea, the Kwoma and Nukuma people celebrate the yam harvest with a similar ceremony. They carve wooden sculptures in the form of the spirit Yena, and they may fashion them as a human head on a long spike.

A Papua New Guinean wooden shelter is used to house the precious crop of yams.

A Kwoma mask features Yena, a spirit connected with the yam harvest festivities.

Vanuatu Yam Harvest

The Vanuatu Islands, north of New Zealand, have many traditional ritual events. Festivities to celebrate the yam harvest have always been one of the most important. Singing and dancing is integral to the harvest celebration, and a special song is always performed to secure a good yam harvest.

An Abelam ceremonial house is richly decorated with wood carvings and paintings of ancestor spirits.

Ceremonial Houses

The Abelam people of Papua New Guinea share many myths with the other cultures of the island. The outside of their ceremonial house is decorated with painted faces of spirits. During initiation or harvest ceremonies, the inside is decorated with wooden carvings and paintings of ancestors. Some carvings are so long and heavy that two people are needed to carry them. During the festival, yams are decorated with masks, flowers, fruit, and leaves until they resemble humans and are then exchanged among the Abelam people.

Men perform the traditional yam dance on Malakula Island, one of the many islands in the Vanuatu region of Oceania.

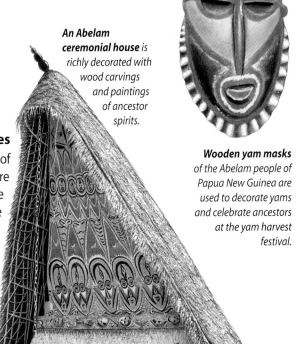

Wooden yam masks of the Abelam people of Papua New Guinea are used to decorate yams and celebrate ancestors at the yam harvest festival.

Glossary

Agriculture The science, art, or occupation of cultivating the soil to make crops grow and of raising farm animals.

Altar A table or raised platform on which offerings are placed, usually found in churches or temples.

Ancestor A family member from a preceding generation to whom you are directly related, for example, a grandfather or great-grandfather.

Blessing Divine favor or protection.

Brewery The place or building where beer is made.

Ceremony The celebration of an important event with an act or series of acts that follow a set of instructions established by a religion, culture, or country.

Colony A group of people who leave their own country and settle in another land but remain citizens of their own country.

Constellation A group of stars with fixed positions that form an imaginary shape in the sky.

Cornhusk The covering of coarse leaves enclosing an ear of corn.

Crop A large number of plants of any given kind that are grown for human use.

Cultivate To prepare and use land to raise crops by plowing it, planting seeds, and taking care of the growing plants.

Culture A way of life. Every human society has a culture that includes its arts, beliefs, customs, institutions, inventions, language, technology, and values.

Deity A god or goddess.

Devout To be active in worship; religious.

Divine Sacred, being related to a god or goddess.

Dwelling A building used as a home or shelter.

Equinox Either of the two days of the year when the sun is directly above Earth's equator. On these days, day and night are of nearly equal length everywhere on Earth. The equinoxes occur on March 19, 20, or 21 and on September 22 or 23.

Fast To choose to go without eating for a time for religious reasons.

Fertility The ability to produce and reproduce things. Land is fertile when many crops can grow there.

Fortune Happiness or good luck that happens in a person's life.

Furrow A narrow trench made in the ground by a plow and in which seeds are planted.

Harvest The reaping and gathering of grain and other food crops.

Israelites The name by which the ancient Jews were known. Israelites were descendants of Abraham's son Jacob, who was also known as Israel.

Jews Descendants of an ancient people called the Hebrews or Israelites.

Livestock Animals, usually cows and sheep, kept and raised for their produce.

Lunar month The period of time from one new moon to the next, which is about 28 days or 4 weeks.

Masquerade A gathering of people wearing masks and costumes to celebrate a special event or occasion.

Mock To make fun of a person or thing by imitation or a particular action.

Monsoon season The rainy season in India and southern Asia, which is accompanied by high winds.

Mortar A cup-shaped bowl usually made of stone or marble, containing food ingredients that are to be ground or beaten.

Muslim A person who follows the religion of Islam.

Pagan A person who is not, for example, a Christian, Jew, or Muslim and who may worship many gods or no god. Modern pagans practice some forms of ancient religions.

Pageant A procession or ceremony to celebrate a special event.

Pestle An instrument used to beat or press a food, such as yams.

Pilgrims Early English settlers of New England, many of whom were members of the group of English Protestants known as Puritans.

Principle A truth or belief that is a foundation for other truths.

Procession A parade held for a religious ceremony or ritual.

Prosperity The condition of having good luck and success.

Purification The act of cleansing a person or object, often through ceremony or ritual.

Recite To say something, such as a prayer or verse, to an audience or in a group of people.

Resemble To look like or be like another person or thing.

Ripen The stage at which a fruit or grain reaches full development and is ready for use.

Ritual A set of repeated actions done in a precise way with a special religious meaning or significance.

Sacrifice The killing of an animal, which is offered to a god or gods as part of worship.

Scarce Being restricted in quantity or amount.

Sheaf One of the bundles in which grain is bound after harvesting.

Shelter A structure that protects from wind, rain, sun, or danger and is used as a temporary home.

Solar calendar A calendar that marks the passing of years by measuring the time it takes Earth to revolve completely around the sun, about 365 and one-quarter days. The Julian calendar, established by Julius Caesar in 46 B.C., and the Gregorian calendar, established by Pope Gregory XIII in 1582, are two examples.

Solstice A time of year at the halfway mark between the two equinoxes, when the sun is at its northernmost or southenmost position in the sky. There are two solstices in a year. In the Northern Hemisphere the summer solstice occurs June 20, 21, or 22, and the winter solstice occurs on December 21 or 22.

Sponsor A person or organization who takes responsibility for a person or thing or provides financial support for an event.

Staple Something of primary importance among a community, such as a particular food or crop.

Starvation The condition of having insufficient food to continue living.

Sumptuous A word describing a building or object produced at great cost with a magnificent, luxurious appearance.

Symbolize To stand for or represent.

Synagogue A Jewish house of worship and a center of Jewish education and social life.

Torah The Hebrew name for the first five books of the Bible.

Tradition The handing down of beliefs, opinions, customs, and stories from generation to generation by word of mouth, or by practice.

Index